I0529995

Published in Canada by Adultbrain Publishing, a division of Grimerica Inc, Calgary.
Adultbrain is a trademark of Grimerica Inc.

Adultbrain books are available at large quantity special discounts. signed copies and audio versions may also be available. For more information contact publishing@adultbrain.ca

Grimes, Darren

Unlearned: Why School Failed You and What to Do About It / by Darren Grimes

1. Self- Help        2. Personal Growth      3. Success
Title: Unlearned

*ISBN 978-1-998704-90-3*
*eISBN 978-1-998704-91-0*

Printed in Canada

Book Design: Adultbrain Publishing
Jacket Design: Adultbrain Publishing

2025
First Edition

# Contents

# Introduction

**This Book Isn't for Everyone.**

It's not for people who want to stay numb, complain about the system, or keep blaming everyone else while their potential collects dust.

It's for those who feel the tension—that itch in your gut that says, *"There's more to me than this."*
It's for the ones who know deep down that they were never taught how to actually live—only how to obey.

School didn't prepare you for the real world. It trained you for a controlled one.
It taught memorization instead of motivation.
Compliance instead of curiosity.
Fear of failure instead of power through practice.

You might've been labeled lazy. Or average. Or unmotivated.
But what if it wasn't you?
What if you were just never taught how to win?

---

## Nothing Is Set in Stone

Let me be clear: **you can change your life at any age**.
There's no expiration date on discipline, purpose, or reinvention.
You could be 15 or 50—what matters is your *decision* to turn the wheel.

But if you're reading this and you're young—**start now.** Because every year you wait, the habits get heavier. The lies get louder. The regret grows deeper.

Starting early doesn't make the path easier. It makes it *yours*.

---

**You Didn't Fail the System—It Failed You**

This book isn't about whining. It's about **reclaiming control.**

You'll learn the stuff that should've been taught in school:

- How your habits shape your identity
- Why discipline isn't punishment—it's power
- How to deal with pressure, addiction, failure, and indecision
- How to build wealth, self-respect, and a name that means something

You'll learn how to stop drifting. How to choose your direction and become the kind of person who leads—without waiting for permission.

This book won't solve your problems. **You will.**
But it will give you the tools.
And the map.
And the mindset.

## It's Time to Unlearn

Unlearn the fear.
Unlearn the self-doubt.
Unlearn the comfort trap they wrapped around your
potential like a blanket.

This is the blueprint you never got.
Read it.
Use it.
Then build something so real and undeniable, no one
can ever put you back in that box again.

Welcome to *Unlearned*.
Let's go.

# Chapter 1: Wake Up Now — Your Next 10 Years Decide Everything

*"The chains of habit are too light to be felt until they are too heavy to be broken."*
—Warren Buffett

You're not a kid anymore.

But you're not a full adult either.

You're in the middle zone—the one where people make or break their lives. Most waste this decade. They drift, numb out, or follow the herd. Then they hit 25 and panic, wondering why their life feels like a trap.

No one tells you this, but it's true:

**The time between 15 and 25 decides the rest of your life.**

That's not poetic. That's reality. What you do, think, repeat, eat, build, and watch right now will shape who you are at 25—and that version of you is either a weapon or a warning.

This isn't about being rich or famous. It's about becoming *free*.

Free to choose your life instead of reacting to someone else's.

Free to trust yourself because you've done hard things.

Free to stand apart from the crowd because you didn't clone your identity from TikTok or YouTube shorts.

You're building something right now, whether you know it or not.
You might as well make it powerful.

---

## Momentum Is Real — And You're Already Moving

You don't need to be perfect. You just need to stop drifting.

Drifting is quiet. It's easy. And it's deadly.

It's when you don't choose—so life chooses for you.
One more skipped workout. One more late-night scroll. One more "I'll do it later."

Nothing breaks. So you think you're okay.

But momentum kicks in. Good or bad.

Habits stack. So does avoidance.

By 25, you'll either be standing on top of a pile of wins— or buried under ten years of small lies you told yourself.

Let's say it out loud: **15 to 25 is the runway. You either build wings, or you crash in slow motion.**

---

**You Are Not "Finding" Yourself — You're Programming Yourself**

Forget the lie that your identity just magically reveals itself. It doesn't.

You build it.

Every single decision right now wires your brain in a direction:

- Start lifting weights? Your body starts believing you're strong.

- Start reading books? Your mind starts believing you're disciplined.

- Stop numbing with weed and porn? Your soul starts remembering it's not meant to escape reality—it's meant to shape it.

You're writing your future self's code. You are both the programmer and the hardware.

Repeat weak habits = weak identity.

Repeat strong ones = you become lethal.

| DRIFTER vs. DRIVEN | |
| --- | --- |
| **Drifter** | **Driven** |
| • Sleeps in<br>• Scrolls endlessly<br>• Avoids discomfort<br>• Blames others<br>• Lives in reaction | • Wakes early<br>• Chooses inputs<br>• Leans into hard things<br>• Owns mistakes<br>• Lives by design |

**Compound Time Effect — The Greatest (and Most Ignored) Law**

Let's say you start reading 10 pages a day right now.

That's 3,650 pages a year.

Do that for 10 years and you've read 36,500 pages—hundreds of books. You've taught your brain how to learn, how to focus, how to think. That alone puts you ahead of 99% of people your age.

Or you skip it. You scroll. You chill. You "wait until later."

But later never gives you a second chance to compound time.

You can catch up—but now you're dragging a decade of mental garbage behind you.

You either let time **compound in your favor**, or let it **compound against you**.

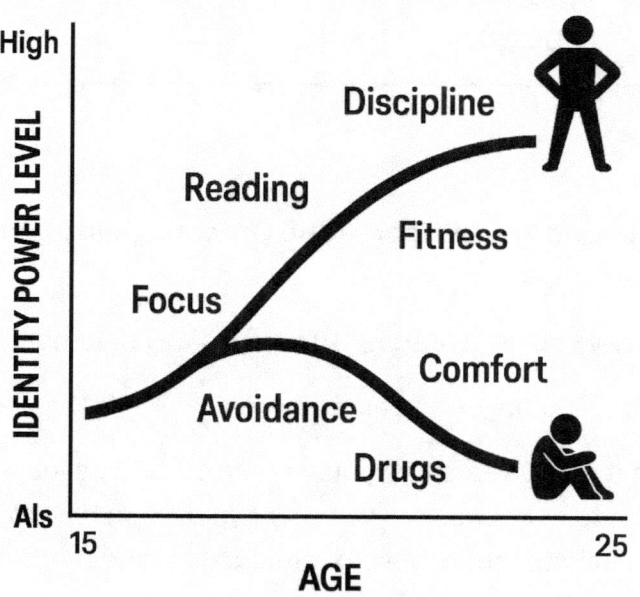

# 10-YEAR MOMENTUM CURVE

## Trap Alert: The Lie That You Have Time

If you're 16 and you say, "I'll figure it out later," congratulations—you've joined the club of people who *never* figure it out.

There are 30-year-olds stuck in jobs they hate because they wasted the compounding years. They weren't dumb. They weren't bad. They just drifted. A year became two. A slump became a lifestyle.

You either build your life on purpose—or life builds it for you.

And life's default setting is: mediocre, broke, tired, resentful.

**The Rule of Identity Formation**

Here's what you were never taught in school:

**You become the person you practice being.**

You're not waiting to discover yourself. You're reinforcing someone every time you act—or avoid acting.

The more you scroll, the more you become a scroller.

The more you lift, the more you become someone who trains.

The more you build, the more you see yourself as a builder.

The more you drift, the more your future self has to fight to undo the damage.

You are not fixed. But you are *forming*.

---

**Legend Lesson**

- The time from 15 to 25 is where destiny gets decided.

- Habits don't just affect outcomes—they *become* identity.

- Drift is invisible at first, but it leads to heavy regret.

## Mind Hack

Write down the name of your "future self" at 25. Give them traits:

- What do they look like?
- What do they do every morning?
- What are they known for?

Now act today like you're auditioning for that role.

That's how you speed-run transformation.

## Trap Alert

Drifting feels safe. That's the trick.

It's not safe. It's slow death with a screen and a couch.

# Chapter 2: The Drift Is Real — And It's Coming for You

"The majority of people begin to drift as soon as they meet with opposition, and not one out of ten thousand will keep on trying after failing two or three times."

=Napoleon Hill

**Drift is not sleep. It's hypnosis.**

It feels calm. Soft. Easy.

You're not in pain. But you're also not in control. You're not choosing. You're reacting.
That's the danger of the drift—it *feels* harmless. But it's quietly turning you into a person you didn't choose to be.

Napoleon Hill said it like this:
**"Drifting is the habit of letting yourself be tossed around by circumstances, opinions, and distractions—without purpose or resistance."**

That's exactly what most of the world is doing.

Drifting isn't laziness. It's worse.
Drifting is doing *just enough* to avoid the consequences, but never enough to build anything real.
It's the illusion of movement with zero destination.

## What Drifting Looks Like Today

Let's not pretend this is 1937.

Today's drift has a new name: the **algorithm**.

If you wake up and check your phone before you check in with yourself, the algorithm is your god. It decides your inputs, your moods, your thoughts. That TikTok you watched at 9:03 a.m.? It shifted your dopamine baseline for the whole day. The ad you swiped past? It whispered what kind of body or lifestyle you should worship.

If you don't deliberately aim your life, **you'll get fed a life someone else profits from.**

---

## How the Drift Gets in

### 1. Peer Pressure
You want to stand out, but you also don't want to get laughed at. You want to be respected, but you also want to belong. This is the sweet spot where the drift thrives: the fear of being different.

So you stop trying. You dress like them. Speak like them. Joke like them. Think like them. Scroll what they scroll.

You become a clone with a beating heart—and that heart is getting weaker.

### 2. Indecision
Should I get a job or not?

Should I apply or wait?
Should I write this song, start that thing, risk that move?

*Drift lives in the pause.* You think you're being cautious, but what you're actually doing is giving away your power. The longer you wait, the harder it gets to start. And life starts filling in the blanks for you. Usually with garbage.

### 3. Algorithm Addiction

Every time you open a screen without purpose, you step into someone else's story. The drift disguises itself as "just one video," "just checking my feed," or "just winding down." But really? You're outsourcing your mind.

You're drifting into someone else's world—and when you come back, you've forgotten what you were building.

---

### You're Always Being Programmed

There's no neutral.

You're either building yourself—or being built by something else.

That means you don't have the option to do nothing. Even when you do "nothing," you're still training your brain. And most of the time, you're training it to be weaker.

- Every skipped workout programs comfort.

- Every mindless scroll trains distraction.

- Every avoided conversation installs fear.

Eventually, you wake up wondering why you're anxious, lazy, and lost—and it's because *you trained yourself* to be that way.

# DRIFTER vs. DRIVEN

| DRIFTER | DRIVEN |
| --- | --- |
| I don't know what to do... | I'll figure it out by trying |
| Waits for motivation | Acts before it feels easy |
| Blames the algorithm, system, school | Builds despite all of them |
| Addicted to comfort | Addicted to growth |
| Numbs out with weed, porn, food | Builds energy with movement |
| Follows the crowd | Defines their own path |
| Obsessed with how they look | Obsessed with who they are |
| Distracted | Dialed-in |

## The Drift Costs You the Most Important Thing

**Time.**

Every day you drift, you lose something you'll never get back.

Not just minutes on the clock—but *compound interest on your potential*.

Think of your life like a rocket. Every week of drifting is a delay in launch.
But it's not just delay—it's damage. The longer you wait, the more repair you'll need.
The more bad habits form. The more your confidence erodes.
The more you convince yourself you're "just not that type of person."

Here's the truth: you were. You just drifted too long.

---

### Legend Lesson

- The world will always choose comfort and mediocrity for you. It's your job to reject it.

- Drift is deadly because it doesn't *feel* dangerous.

- You are never doing nothing—you are either building or breaking.

**Mind Hack**

Write down three things you do every day without thinking.

Now ask:

- Are these strengthening me or weakening me?
- Would my 25-year-old self thank me for these habits?

Cut one. Replace it with something simple and strong.

---

**Trap Alert**

Every second you don't choose your life, someone else's script loads in the background.
It's written by corporations, distractions, and peer pressure.
And it *never* ends in greatness.

# Chapter 3: Hard Work Is the Real Flex

"The only place success comes before work is in the dictionary."
— Vince Lombardi

Everyone wants the outcome.
No one wants the reps.

Everyone wants the attention.
Few want the grind that earns respect.

But let me let you in on a secret: **hard work is the cheat code.**
It's not cringe. It's not outdated. It's not something to apologize for.

It's elite.
And in a world of shortcuts, comfort, and fake effort, **real work is rebellion.**

---

**Why Work Ethic Beats Talent**

Let's kill the myth right now: **talent is overrated**.

Being naturally good at something means nothing if you never train it.
The hardest workers in the room will eventually outgrow the gifted kids—because while the gifted coast, the grinders evolve.

You've seen this happen.

- The kid who was amazing at sports but stopped trying and washed out.
- The one who was naturally smart but never studied and now barely scrapes by.
- The guy who was good-locking in high school but never built anything, now posting gym selfies with zero direction.

**Talent without effort is potential wasted.**
Effort without talent? That's the beginning of something unstoppable.

---

**Nobody Regrets the Work—Only the Lack of It**

You never finish a hard workout and wish you skipped it. You never finish writing, practicing, reading, lifting, or building and think, "That was a waste."

But scroll for three hours? Get high alone again?
You finish that and feel smaller.

That's the difference.

Hard work builds *internal gravity*. You respect yourself more.
And when you respect yourself, you stop tolerating average—*from others and from yourself.*

---

**Every Rep You Put In Buys You Freedom**

Let's talk about the trade no one explains:

**You can suffer now and earn freedom later. Or escape now and live in a cage later.**

That's it. That's the formula.

Work is the tax you pay for greatness.
And if you avoid it, you're just delaying the bill—and interest stacks.

When you put in reps:

- You build discipline.

- You create options.

- You unlock energy.

- You magnetize better friends, relationships, opportunities.

- You get used to *winning* instead of waiting.

# EFFORT-TO-REWARD RATIO PYRAMID

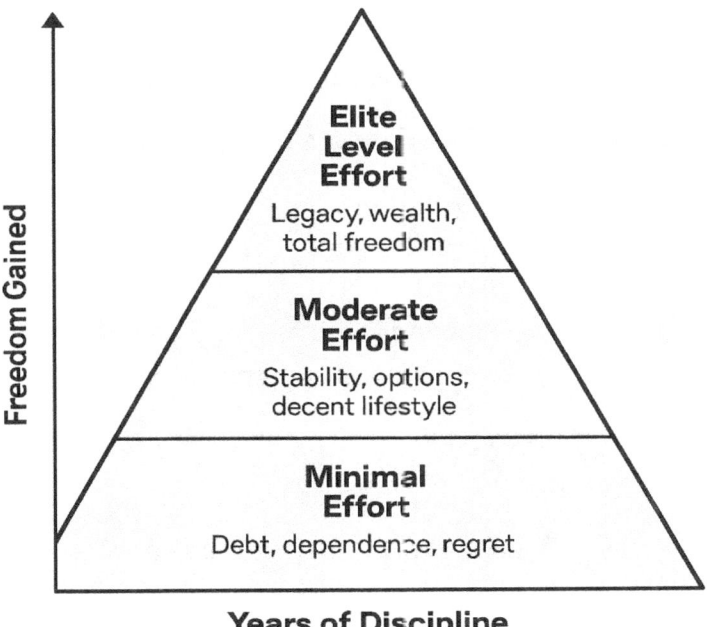

Freedom Gained

**Elite Level Effort**
Legacy, wealth, total freedom

**Moderate Effort**
Stability, options, decent lifestyle

**Minimal Effort**
Debt, dependence, regret

**Years of Discipline**

The steeper the climb,
the better the view.

# Chapter 4: Alcohol, Weed, and the Slow Death of Potential

"Drugs and alcohol steal ambition, crush resolve, and trade your future for a moment's escape."

-Jim Rohn

Nobody wants to talk about this. So let's talk about it.

**The truth is: most people are numbing.**

Not partying. Not exploring. Not relaxing.

**Numbing.**

That's what alcohol and weed are for most people— coping tools, not conscious choices.

They say "I just do it to unwind." Translation: *I can't handle my own mind sober.*

They say "It's just for fun." Translation: *Life feels boring unless I'm altered.*

They say "I'm in control." Translation: *I'm scared of stopping and facing my shit.*

The lie is that it's harmless.
The truth is, it's weakening you. Not all at once. But little by little, until the spark in you is gone.

---

**This Isn't About Morality — It's About Power**

You can believe whatever you want about drugs and alcohol. This isn't about rules.
It's about *results*.

Ask yourself this:

- Are you sharper after smoking?

- Are you hungrier to win after drinking?

- Are you clearer, stronger, more focused after numbing out?

Didn't think so.

**Every time you numb, you dull the blade.**

And your brain remembers.

---

**The "Fuck-It" Mindset Trap**

There's a dangerous moment that happens right before most people light up or pour another drink.

It sounds like this:

"Screw it. I'll get back on track tomorrow."

"It's not like I'm doing anything important tonight anyway."

"I deserve it. It's been a hard day."

That's the *fuck-it* mindset. And it's the beginning of a slippery spiral.

Because *fuck-it* turns into *f-it again tomorrow,* then *f-it this week,* then *who even cares anymore.*

This is how the strongest people become shadows of who they could have been.

One small *fuck-it* at a time.

---

**The Neural Cost of Escapism**

Let's talk brain science—quick and simple.

When you get high or drunk:

- Your brain floods with artificial dopamine.

- Your body feels good. But your mind isn't learning how to generate that good feeling naturally.

- Over time, your dopamine baseline lowers. Meaning you feel *less motivated, less excited, less capable* doing regular things.

Translation?
You stop feeling like doing the hard stuff—the gym, the writing, the hustle, the growth.

And that's when you start thinking: *maybe I'm just not that driven.*
But it's not you—it's your chemistry.

You trained your brain to feel *only* when numbing.

That's why you feel stuck.

# BRAIN POWER DRAIN METER

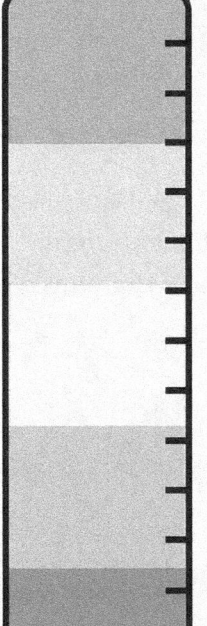

🔥 **PEAK**
focused, clear,
explosive creativity

**FUNCTIONAL**
stable but passive

**FLATLINE**
bored, reactive, avoidant

**DULL**
lazy, confused, moody

**BURNT OUT**
no focus, no ambition
no emotion

Daily weed/alcohol = drop
1–2 levels over time

Extended sobriety = climb the scale

**EVERY CHOICE REWIRES YOUR BRAIN. FEED POWER OR+ WEAKNESS**

## Why They Want You Numb

Here's the hard truth: **the system prefers you doped up.**

- Numb people don't challenge anything.

- Numb people buy dumb shit.

- Numb people stay stuck in loops.

- Numb people never build anything threatening to the status quo.

They say it's liberation. They say it's your right.
And it is. But just remember: **a free man who's numb is easier to enslave.**

---

## You Can Still Party Without Poison

Want to feel free? Hype? Alive?

Try this:

- Workout so hard you feel high on your own sweat.

- Create something that keeps you up all night.

- Learn a skill that flips your confidence switch.

- Build a crew of people who sharpen you, not sedate you.

That's the real drug.
**That's the real buzz.**

---

**Legend Lesson**

- Numbing now kills your drive later.

- You don't need to be perfect—but you need to be *present*.

- Your potential doesn't die in one overdose. It dies in 1,000 tiny numbing rituals.

---

**Mind Hack**

Go 30 days sober.
Not because you "have a problem."
But because you want to *prove* to yourself that you own your brain—not the other way around.

Journal your energy levels every 5 days. Watch what happens.

---

**Trap Alert**

"Just this once" is the trap door that leads to "this is who I am now."

# Chapter 5: You Are What You Watch, Scroll, and Repeat

"Your attention is the most important asset. Where you spend it determines who you are."

-Naval Ravikant

Let's get real: your phone is not just a device.
It's a training system. And every time you scroll, **you're programming your brain**.

You are not "killing time."
Time is killing *you*—while you let your brain get rewired by whatever trend, fake drama, or brain rot is trending that hour.

Here's the truth:

**Your inputs = your identity.**

What you consume consistently becomes how you think, what you feel, and even *what you believe*.

So, what's on your daily content menu?

---

**The Dopamine Hijack**

Your brain is wired to chase rewards. That's dopamine's job. It says:

- "That felt good—do it again."

- "That gave me attention—repeat it."

- "That gave me escape—come back tomorrow."

Now ask yourself: where is most of your dopamine going?

- Viral videos that make you laugh but leave you hollow?

- Fake flex culture that makes you compare and spiral?

- Influencers selling you rage, outrage, or envy for clicks?

**That's your dopamine being hijacked.**
Not for your benefit—but for *profit*.

And the scariest part? Your brain adapts to it.

It gets bored of real life.
It becomes numb to effort.
It starts craving fake stimulation over real progress.

This is how the algorithm traps you—*not by force, but by repetition*.

---

## Your Feed Is a Mirror—But Also a Cage

Ever noticed how TikTok and Instagram "know" what you want?
That's not magic. That's addiction science. Machine-learning personalization.

But what you don't realize is this:

**It doesn't just show you what you want. It shows you what keeps you weak.**

- Addicted to hot-take content? You'll stay angry but unfocused.

- Obsessed with beauty standards? You'll stay insecure.

- Chasing perfect bodies? You'll hate your own and never feel enough.

- Watching "day in the life" hustle montages? You'll feel behind—no matter what.

The algorithm is designed to keep you watching.
And if your mental health suffers? They don't care. They got the view.

# MENTAL DIET TRACKER

## JUNK INPUT

 Mindless TikToks

 Toxic celebrity culture

 Influencer perfection

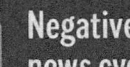 Negative news cycles

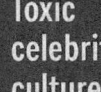
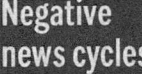

## VALUE INPUT

 Sovereign Indigenous teachings

 Real-world wisdom

 Experiential knowledge

Growth challenges

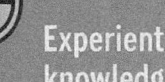

### EMOTIONAL EFFECTS

Upset     Insecure

### COGNITIVE EFFECTS

Scattered focus     Powerless

### EMOTIONAL EFFECTS

Focused     Inspired

### COGNITIVE EFFECTS

Clear mind     Self-empowered

 **THEY USE YOUR FRUSTRATION.**
**CHOOSE TO TAKE BACK YOUR FUTURE.**

**Beliefs Are Planted in Your Feed**

Your brain can't help but absorb patterns.

Watch enough relationship drama? You start distrusting people.
Watch enough political rage clips? You start thinking the world is hopeless.
Watch enough fake perfection? You start hating your real life.

Your beliefs didn't come from deep reflection.
They came from **repetition.**

And repetition is controlled by *your feed*.

---

**What You Watch Is What You Worship**

If your life sucks, your self-esteem is shot, and you don't know why—start with your content diet.

Ask:

- Do I follow people who sharpen me? Or sedate me?

- Do I watch things that build me? Or break me?

- Would I be proud if my future self saw my "For You" page?

This isn't about being perfect. It's about being *conscious*.

## Legend Lesson

- Your inputs shape your identity, mood, and beliefs.

- Algorithms don't care about your potential—only your attention.

- You are either watching your future grow—or your power drain.

## Mind Hack

Delete or unfollow **5 accounts** that make you feel worse after watching them.

Replace them with **5 voices** that teach, push, or sharpen you.

Every scroll trains your brain.
So train for greatness—not garbage.

## Trap Alert

If you don't control your content, your content will control you.

And it never leads to freedom. Just sedation with a bright screen.

# Chapter 6: Be the Hero — Not a Victim, Not a Clone

*"The man who does not value himself, cannot value anything or anyone."*

-Ayn Rand

There are three types of people in this world.

You've seen them. You know them.

Hell, maybe you've been all three.

Let's break them down.

---

## 1. The Victim

The Victim believes the world is against them.
That everything bad is someone else's fault.

They say:

- "It's not fair."

- "I can't because of my past."

- "Nobody helped me."

And you know what? Sometimes, they're right.
Life *isn't* fair. Some people *do* get dealt a worse hand.

But here's the problem: **Victims stop there.**
They sit in it. They stew in it. And eventually, it becomes their identity.

Victims don't build.
They beg.
They complain.
They wait for someone to save them.

And they die bitter.

---

## 2. The Clone

The Clone doesn't blame anyone. They don't even think that much.
They just *copy.*

Whatever's trending—*they wear it.*
Whatever the group says—*they agree.*
Whatever gets likes—*they do that too.*

They're not bad people. They're just... empty.

Clones don't know what they believe.
They're scared to be different.
So they chase safety, acceptance, and aesthetics.

You don't notice a clone until they're gone—because they never made an impact.

---

## 3. The Hero

The Hero isn't perfect. They're not even always right.

But they *own their path*.

Heroes know no one's coming to save them.
So they become their own rescue plan.

Heroes don't need permission.
They build.
They try.
They bleed.
They get knocked down and get back up louder.

The Hero archetype is in every culture, every era, every story for a reason.

It's *you*—if you choose it.

# Three Paths

Victim     Clone     Hero

# Destiny is built, not inherited.

### Radical Ownership = Freedom

The moment you take full responsibility for your life—
even the bad shit—you unlock your power.

This doesn't mean it's all your fault.
It means it's all your *move*.

That's radical ownership.

And it's the single biggest mindset difference between
winners and whiners.

Victims need the system to change.
Clones need others to go first.
**Heroes change themselves—and then change the world.**

---

**Effort Over Entitlement**

You're not owed success.
You're not owed attention.
You're not owed understanding, fairness, or rewards.

You *earn* those through action.

Think about it:

- You don't deserve respect—you show up like someone who demands it.

- You don't deserve freedom—you build it.

- You don't deserve a platform—you earn trust, prove value, and speak truth.

Entitlement says: "Why don't I have it?"
Effort says: "Let me go earn it."

One gets you nowhere. The other gets you *everything*.

---

**Legend Lesson**

- Victim = blame. Clone = copy. Hero = build.

- Radical ownership gives you leverage over your life.

- You don't need to be perfect—you just need to take the wheel.

---

## Mind Hack

Take one part of your life that's bothering you—school, work, body, confidence.
Ask: *What would the Hero version of me do here—today?*

Now do *any small piece* of that.

It doesn't have to be perfect. It just has to be *yours*.

---

## Trap Alert

If you wait for fairness, you'll wait forever.
If you wait for others, you'll follow forever.

Build anyway. Walk anyway.
**Be the hero. Or be forgotten.**

# Chapter 7: Energy, Ethics, and the Law of Compounding

*"The successful warrior is the average man, with laser-like focus."*

-Bruce Lee

Let's talk about the real game-changer: **energy.**

Not just calories. Not just willpower.

We're talking about the power you walk into a room with.
Your mood. Your drive. Your ability to focus, speak, lead, attract, and create.

That's energy.

And here's the truth no one teaches you:
**Energy is currency.**

Spend it right—you get richer.
Waste it—you go broke.

And just like money, **it compounds**.

---

## You Are Either Charging or Draining

Every single action you take today does one of two things:

- Adds fuel to your system

- Leaks fuel from your system

That's it. No neutral.

Let's break this down:

## Upward Fuel Loop

- Clean food = stable mood
- Deep sleep = clean brain
- Morning workout = momentum
- Honest action = peace of mind
- Clear goals = focused drive
- Gratitude = emotional stability

## Downward Drain Loop

- Sugar, junk, caffeine overload = energy crash
- Doomscrolling = anxiety and dopamine burnout
- Lying or half-assing = shame and low self-trust
- Porn, weed, and shortcuts = low emotional voltage
- Complaining = mental clutter
- Distraction = energy hemorrhage

You don't need to be perfect.

But if most of your day is in the **drain zone**, don't be shocked when your life feels flat.

# DAILY ENERGY INVESTMENT WHEEL

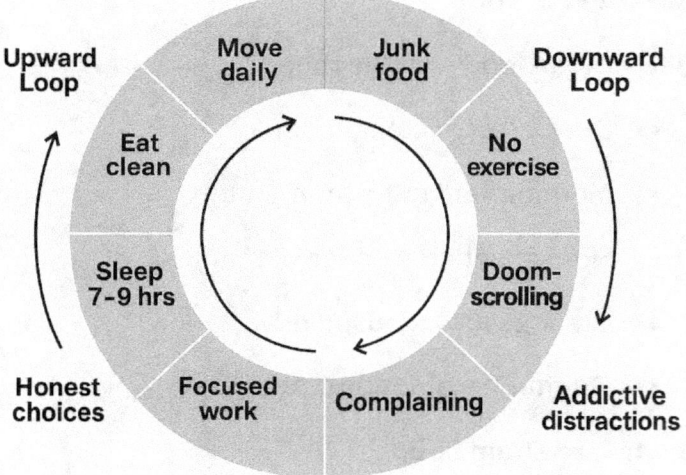

**Energy is built or burned—loop by loop.**

## What You Do = Who You Attract

Want to be around stronger, wiser, clearer people?

You have to *become* one.

People can feel your energy.
Your vibe is the sum total of your choices.

- Integrity makes you magnetic.

- Chaos makes you repellent.

- Focus makes you a force.

- Drama makes you a drain.

That's not "spiritual" talk. That's real life. That's physics.

You attract what you broadcast.
Your energy is the frequency your life tunes to.

---

## Why Ethics Aren't Optional

Want more energy? Start by being honest.

With others. But more importantly—with yourself.

- Did you do what you said you'd do?

- Are you hiding things?

- Do you cut corners, exaggerate, lie to avoid discomfort?

Every ethical shortcut is a leak in your tank.
You might save face in the moment—but you lose force in the long run.

**Real strength is built on self-trust.**
And self-trust is built by living in alignment.

---

## Compounding Is the Unseen King

Do something weak once? No big deal.
Do it every day? You've just programmed your identity.

Do something strong once? A win.
Do it daily? You've built a weapon.

This is the law of compounding. It's slow. Boring. Invisible.

But in five years, you'll either thank your former self—or be begging for a reset you can't have.

---

**Legend Lesson**

- Your energy is your edge—and you choose to fuel or drain it.

- Your integrity *is* your magnetism.

- Compounding doesn't care if you're building or breaking—it just multiplies.

---

**Mind Hack**

Choose **3 upward energy behaviors** and **3 downward drains** from the wheel.

Track them for 7 days—tick a box every time you do one.

At the end, ask:
*Which version of me am I compounding?*

---

**Trap Alert**

Energy doesn't disappear.

It gets stolen by distractions—or invested in your mission.

Your habits choose who it serves.

# Chapter 8: Failure Is Fuel, Not a Finish Line

*"Success is stumbling from failure to failure with no loss of enthusiasm."*

-Winston Churchill

You're going to fail.

Over and over.

At stuff that matters.
At stuff you thought you were good at.
In front of people. Alone. At the worst possible moment.

And if you're lucky?
You'll learn to love it.

Because failure isn't punishment.
**It's training.**

---

## The Real Test: Who Comes Back After Falling?

Most people don't fail because they're weak.
They fail because they quit too early.

They take the L and disappear.
They ghost the grind.
They walk away from the gym, the job, the art, the call, the challenge—because it didn't go perfectly the first time.

But here's the hidden rule:

**Everyone fails. The winners just come back swinging.**

You failed? Good.
You got rejected? Perfect.
That means you stepped into the arena. That's rare.

Now comes the question: *What are you going to do with it?*

---

**Failure Isn't the End—It's the Feedback**

Let's rewire the script right now:

- Failure isn't final—it's feedback.

- Rejection isn't rejection—it's redirection.

- Falling isn't weakness—it's weight training for your mind.

You're not supposed to get it right on the first try. That's not how mastery works.

**You fail → you learn → you adjust → you grow.**
Or you fail → get embarrassed → h de → stay stuck.

Your choice.

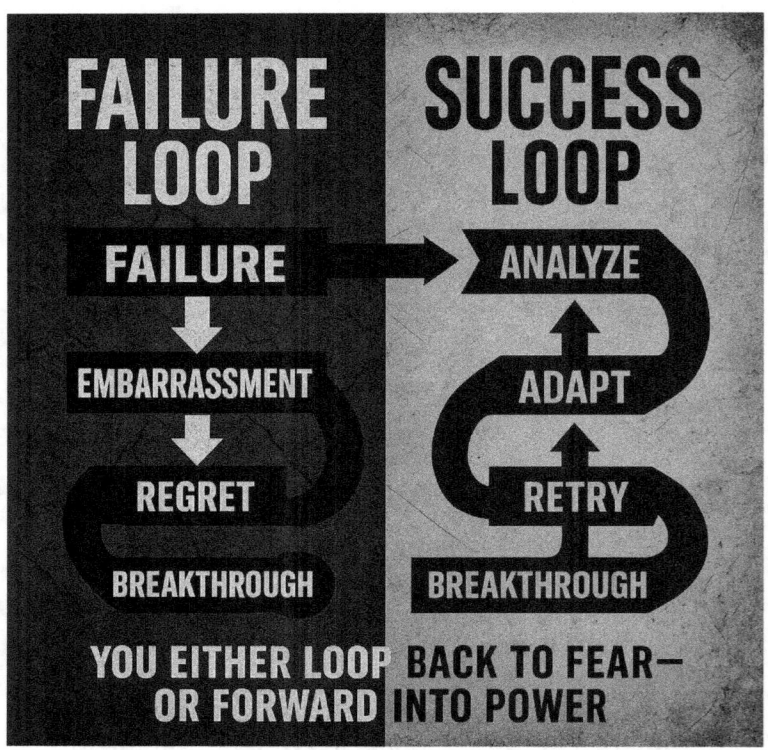

**FAILURE LOOP**
FAILURE → ANALYZE
EMBARRASSMENT
REGRET
BREAKTHROUGH

**SUCCESS LOOP**
ANALYZE
ADAPT
RETRY
BREAKTHROUGH

**YOU EITHER LOOP BACK TO FEAR—OR FORWARD INTO POWER**

### Perfection Is a Lie

One of the biggest traps young people fall into is this:

"If I'm not amazing right away, I shouldn't even try."

That's coward talk.

You don't get confident and *then* take action.
You take action—and *that's how you earn confidence*.

Perfection is a trick your brain uses to protect you from risk.
But perfection never built anything real.
**Persistence did.**

**Fail Loud. Fail Proud. Fail Forward.**

Stop trying to avoid failure.
It's coming anyway. Might as well make it count.

Launch the channel.
Ask the question.
Start the workout.
Apply. Compete. Risk. Fall.

Every failure is fuel—if you collect it and use it.

**Legend Lesson**

- Failure is proof you're playing the real game.

- Quitting builds regret. Persistence builds strength.

- You don't need to be perfect—you just need to return.

**Mind Hack**

Write this on a card or note:

**"My job isn't to win today. My job is to show up and evolve."**

Stick it to your wall, your mirror, your phone case. Read it before every risk.

**Trap Alert**

The world doesn't remember people who *almost* tried.

If you quit after failure, you fail for real.

Keep going.

# Chapter 9: Why No One's Coming to Save You

*"He who is not everyday conquering some fear has not learned the secret of life."*

-Ralph Waldo Emerson

Let's cut straight through the lie:

**No one is coming.**

Not your parents.
Not your teachers.
Not your boss, your coach, your partner, or the universe.
Not the government. Not the algorithm. Not even "future you."

If you're waiting for someone to *make* you successful—stop.

If you're waiting for motivation, confidence, clarity, timing—stop.

You're not waiting for the right time.
You're just avoiding the truth:
**You're the only one who can move your feet.**

---

## The Rescue Fantasy Must Die

Everyone secretly wants the same thing:

- Someone to discover them

- Someone to believe in them

- Someone to fund, fix, lift, or guide them

- A sign. A moment. A message from the sky

And you know what?

You might get one of those.
But if you're not already moving, *none of it will matter.*

The world rewards people who help themselves.
And buries the ones who wait.

## Start Before You're Ready

Here's the ugly truth:

**You will never feel ready.**
You will never feel like the perfect time has arrived.

So what?

Start anyway.

The act of starting **builds clarity**.
The act of risking **builds confidence**.
The act of moving **builds momentum**.

Everyone else is sitting around planning, overthinking, wondering, scrolling.

**Be the one who's already building.**

---

## You Only Get Better By Doing

You don't become a great speaker by reading books about speaking.
You don't become strong by watching workout videos.
You don't build a business by dreaming about someday.

You get good by showing up while you still suck.

So stop strategizing for your "perfect launch."
Stop rehearsing your ideal future.
Start. Today. Clumsy, broke, confused—*start anyway*.

**The Longer You Wait, The Heavier It Gets**

There's one more brutal truth:

**Waiting is suicide—but it's the slow kind.**

Every day you delay the thing you *know* you should start...

- Your confidence erodes
- Your self-trust breaks down
- Your regret builds
- Your fire dies

That thing you're "thinking about doing?"
It will **own you** if you don't build it.

---

**Legend Lesson**

- Waiting is self-sabotage with a polite mask.
- You will never feel ready—but movement creates clarity.
- No one is coming. Build anyway.

---

**Mind Hack**

Ask yourself: *What would I do if I knew no one was going to save me?*

Now do one small version of that.

Send the email. Start the rep. Record the video. Ask the question. Write the first sentence.

Act like **you're the rescue team.** Because you are.

---

**Trap Alert**

If you stay in the waiting room long enough, you forget you can leave.

Don't rot in potential. Build your escape.

# Chapter 10: Your Mind Is a Magnet — So Point It Right

*"Watch your thoughts; they become words.*

*Watch your words; they become actions.*

*Watch your actions; they become habits.*

*Watch your habits; they become character.*

*Watch your character; it becomes your destiny."*

-Lao Tzu

Let's stop pretending this is woo-woo.

Let's stop treating "positive thinking" like it's some cheap self-help mantra.

Here's what's actually happening:

**Your mind is a magnet.**
It pulls in experiences, choices, and outcomes that match what it's tuned to.

If you think like a loser—you'll live like one.
Not because of magic, but because *you'll start making loser-level decisions* without even realizing it.

---

**Thought Is a Program — and You're Running It on Loop**

Everything you do starts with a thought.

- "I'm not good enough."

- "This probably won't work."

- "They won't like me."

- "I always mess this up."

- "Why even bother?"

Say that enough and your brain *believes it*.
And once it believes it, it stops even *trying* to prove you wrong.

You act small. You hide. You play safe. You avoid risk. And the world reflects back exactly what you were expecting: failure, rejection, invisibility.

Not because you were cursed—because *you aimed your magnet at weakness*.

---

**The Loop That Builds Your Life (or Destroys It)**

Let's break this down.

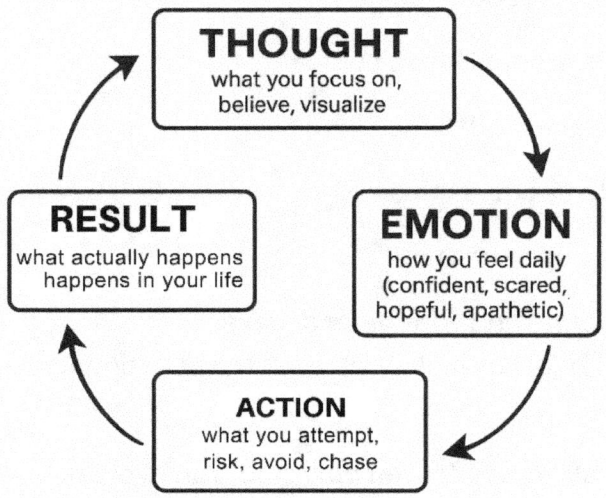

Your identity isn't fixed. It's looped.

### The Science of Visualization (Not Vibes)

Visualization isn't some spiritual ritual.

It's **neural rehearsal.**

Your brain can't fully tell the difference between a vividly imagined act and a real one. That means when you imagine yourself winning—speaking clearly, walking with power, lifting more, succeeding—your brain starts wiring for that reality.

You literally *train your nervous system* before you act.

Elite athletes do it. Special forces operators do it. You should too.

## Thought Hygiene Is Mental Discipline

Just like you brush your teeth to stay clean, you need to clean out toxic thinking.

- Would I say this to someone I love?

- Does this belief serve my future?

- Is this thought based on truth—or fear?

You are not your thoughts.
But if you don't challenge them, you'll *become* them.

This doesn't mean lie to yourself. It means **aim** yourself. You're the one holding the magnet. Point it at power— not poison.

---

## Legend Lesson

- Your brain is always listening to you. Talk like someone who wants to w n.

- Thought becomes emotion. Emotion becomes action. Action becomes identity.

- Don't feed your mind tras¬ and expect your life to feel clean.

---

## Mind Hack

Set a timer for 2 minutes.
Close your eyes.

Picture your highest self doing something specific—strong, focused, unshakable.

See it clearly.
Feel it in your body.
Let it loop.

Then go do one small action that matches that person's vibe.

---

**Trap Alert**

If you don't control your mind, someone else will—through fear, doubt, or distraction.

And you'll build someone else's dream while killing your own.

# Chapter 11: The Discipline Loop — How Habits Build Titans

*"Discipline equals freedom."*

-Jocko Willink

Everyone starts hot.

Day 1: "I'm gonna get shredded."
Day 2: New notebook, new pre-workout, new playlist.
Day 7: Forgotten.
Day 14: Deleted.
Day 21: Back to square one, blaming "laziness."

Here's the problem: You're relying on **hype**.

Motivation is a sugar rush. It disappears when life punches you in the face.

**Discipline is different.**
Discipline doesn't care if you're tired.
Discipline doesn't ask how you feel.
It shows up. Every time.

And it's the only thing that rewires who you are.

---

**The Rule of One**

Most people screw up by doing too much, too fast.

They try to:

- Wake up at 5 AM

- Hit the gym for 2 hours

- Read 50 pages

- Journal, cold shower, meditate, meal prep...

...and they crash by day four.

Forget all that.

**Start with one.**

One habit.
One non-negotiable.
One win you stack daily—even when life sucks.

Do it for 30 days. Then layer another.
This is how titans are built—brick by brick.

---

**Keystone Habits = Identity Anchors**

Some habits matter more than others.
They're called **keystone habits** because they impact everything else.

Here are three that change lives:

- **Wake up early** – Builds structure and pride

- **Exercise daily** – Boosts energy, confidence, sleep, focus

- **Track your day** – Journaling, to-do lists, goal-setting = clarity and momentum

Pick one. Lock it in. Let it evolve your identity.

Because here's the truth:

**You don't rise to the level of your goals—you fall to the strength of your systems.**

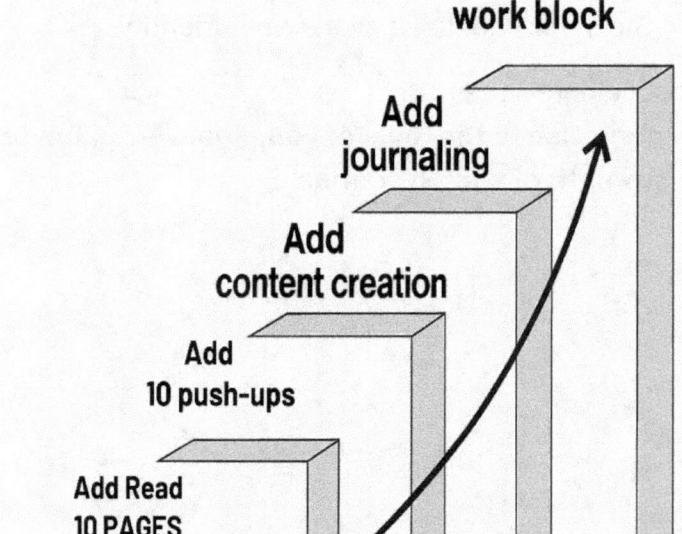

Add deep
work block

Add
journaling

Add
content creation

Add
10 push-ups

Add Read
10 PAGES

Wake
up early

# The Habit Stack Ladder

**Momentum > Motivation**

Once your streak hits 7, 14, 30 days—you *become* the person who does the thing.

It's not hype anymore. It's identity.

Every day you show up, you prove to yourself:

- I'm not weak.

- I follow through.

- I can count on me.

That's power.

You won't always feel like it. Do it anyway.
Because **feeling follows action.**

---

## Legend Lesson

- Habits are the building blocks of your future.

- Discipline beats hype every single time.

- Stack one habit at a time—and become unstoppable.

---

## Mind Hack

Pick **one micro habit** that your future self would already be doing.

Example: 10 push-ups, 1-minute cold shower, 5 pages of reading, no phone before 9AM.

Do it for 7 days. No excuses.
Then layer one more.

Watch how fast your identity evolves.

---

**Trap Alert**

If you don't choose your habits, the algorithm will.

And it won't choose greatness—it'll choose comfort, distraction, and slow decline.

Build your loop. Or get trapped in theirs.

# Chapter 12: Make Money with Integrity or Get Owned by the System

*"You were born to be rich, not to be a wage slave."*

-Wallace Wattles

You want to be free?

Then you need to talk money.
Because here's what nobody's telling you:

**Money is freedom.**
Not greed. Not evil. Just access.
And if you don't earn it on your own terms, you'll trade your time for scraps on someone else's.

---

**The System Buys You Cheap**

Here's how most people sell their soul:

1. Take out loans to chase a "safe" degree they don't care about

2. Get a job that drains them but pays just enough to survive

3. Get a car loan, a credit card, maybe a mortgage

4. Now they can't quit, risk, or build—because they're owned

Congratulations. They're locked into the Matrix.

No time. No leverage. No freedom.

They didn't "fail." They just got bought.

---

**The Side Hustle Is Your Sword**

You don't need a startup or an overnight empire.

You need something that:

- Builds your skills

- Lets you create instead of just consume

- Makes money while you stay in control

Examples:

- Editing, design, writing, tutoring

- Flipping items, trading skills, digital products

- Online services, coaching, gig work with purpose

The goal isn't to flex.
The goal is to **build proof** that you can survive and thrive
without a leash.

# CHAINS vs. WINGS
# MONEY CHART

| CHAINS | WINGS |
|---|---|
| • Credit cards | • Side hustle income |
| • Student loans | • No debt |
| • Paycheck dependence | • Online revenue |
| • Job you hate | • Creating instead of consuming |
| • Spend more than you earn | • Saving & investing |
| → Waiting for raises trapped, anxious, low freedom | → mobility, leverage, time freedom |

**Money is either a leash - or a launchpad.**

**Integrity = Power That Lasts**

Fast cash can wreck you just as fast.

Don't scam. Don't cheat. Don't burn people.

Build slow if you have to—but build with honor.
Because **the way you make money shapes who you become.**

If your name means nothing, your success means nothing.

- Do great work

- Keep your word

- Charge fair and deliver more

- Be the person people trust

In the long run, integrity is the ultimate income stream.

---

**Legend Lesson**

- Money doesn't make you greedy. It makes you **free**—if you earn it right.

- The system's default is debt and chains. Build outside of it.

- Side hustles = skill. Skill = power. Power = options.

---

## Mind Hack

Ask: "How could I trade **creation** for income this month?"

Think: selling, helping, building, teaching, designing, fixing, organizing.

Pick one. Make it real.

Doesn't have to be perfect. Has to be **yours**.

---

## Trap Alert

If your income depends on someone else's permission, you're always one step away from panic.

Build something no one can take.

# Chapter 13: Vision Is the Weapon They Forgot to Give You

*"He who has a why to live can bear almost any how."*

-Friedrich Nietzsche

The easiest people to control are the ones without direction.

- They follow the crowd

- They chase clout

- They copy whatever they see online

- They let their moods pick their future

They're not stupid. They're **visionless**.

And that makes them dangerous to themselves—and useless to others.

Here's the truth:

**Without vision, you drift. With vision, you dominate.**

---

## The Compass in Your Chest

Vision isn't a wish.
It's not just "a goal."
It's a direction. A *code* you carry into battle.

It's what you fight for when you're tired.
What keeps you honest when no one's looking.
What makes you immune to peer pressure, trends, or traps.

Vision doesn't just help you win.
It makes you unshakable.

---

## How to Build a 10-Year Vision

Forget where you're at right now.

Ask:

- Who do I want to be at 25?

- What skills will I have mastered?

- What kind of people will I attract?

- What will my days look like?

- What impact will I be making?

Write it down. In detail.

This is your **10-year map**.
You won't follow it perfectly. But it gives you **north**—and most people have nothing.

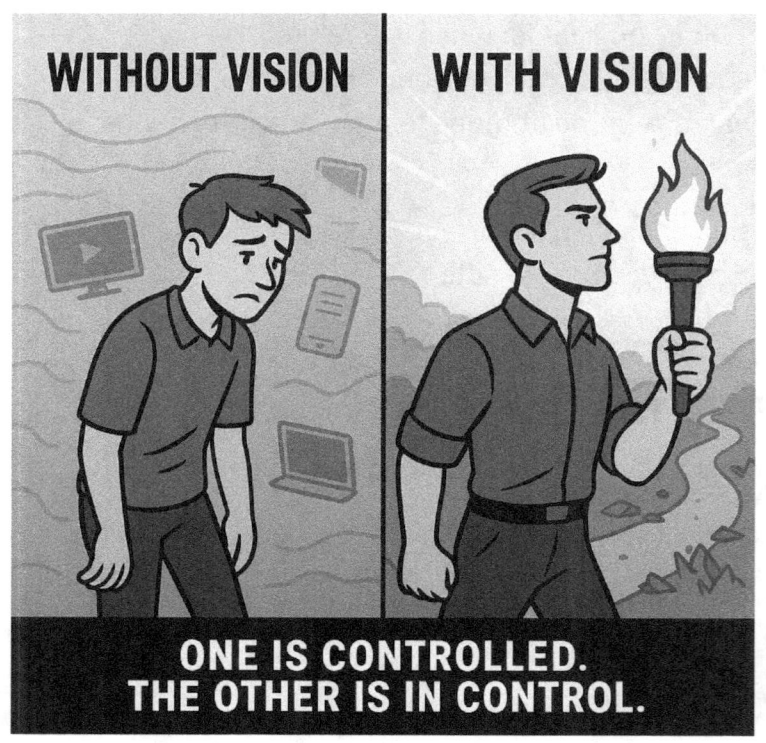

**WITHOUT VISION** | **WITH VISION**

**ONE IS CONTROLLED.**
**THE OTHER IS IN CONTROL.**

**Write Your Personal Manifesto**

What do you stand for?
What won't you tolerate?
What drives you?
What are you building?

Put it on paper. Call it what it is: **your mission**.

When the world throws you nonsense, this is how you say "No thanks. I have work to do."

Most people wait for someone else to give them purpose.
You're going to write your own.

---

## Legend Lesson

- Vision isn't fantasy. It's *armor*.

- You can't be manipulated if you already know where you're going.

- The more vivid your mission, the more powerful your momentum.

---

## Mind Hack

Write your "I am" identity statement as if it's already true.

"I am a skilled, respected builder who creates freedom for myself and others.
I train daily. I speak with power. I move with clarity."

Tape it somewhere you see every morning. Then move like it's real—because it will be.

---

## Trap Alert

If you don't choose your vision, the world will hand you one:
Consume. Obey. Stay confused. Stay small.

Burn that script. Write your own.

# Chapter 14: Legacy Mode — Why You Start Now or Regret Later

*"What you do speaks so loudly that I cannot hear what you say."*

-Ralph Waldo Emerson

There will come a day when your name is spoken for the last time.

When your social media is deleted.
Your clothes donated.
Your phone wiped.
And what's left?

**A legacy—or a question mark.**

---

**You're Not Too Young. You're Right on Time.**

Most people think legacy is for "later."

Wrong.

**Legacy starts now.**
Every habit, every risk, every project, every time you show up when it's easier not to—*that's legacy in motion.*

You're either building something future-you will thank you for...
Or you're building a mountain of regret.

---

**Time: The Only Asset That Matters**

Forget money for a second.
Forget status. Likes. Followers. Hype.

You have one thing that *cannot* be replaced: **time**.

Every minute is either:

- An investment in the story of who you're becoming

- Or a leak that someone else benefits from

Wasting your time isn't "chill." It's theft—from your future self.

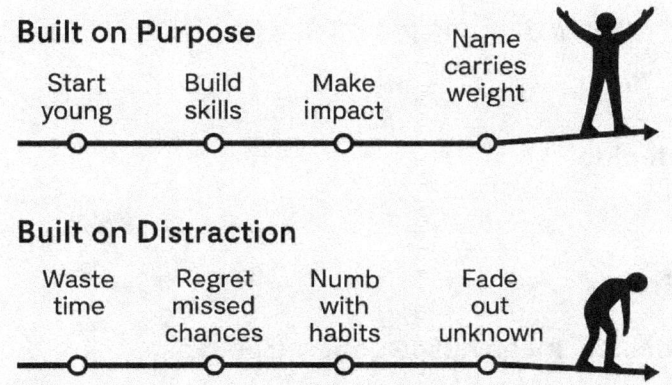

# LEGACY TIMELINE

## Built on Purpose

| Start young | Build skills | Make impact | Name carries weight |
|---|---|---|---|

## Built on Distraction

| Waste time | Regret missed chances | Numb with habits | Fade out unknown |
|---|---|---|---|

**The only way to be remembered is to make your time matter.**

### Your Name Is Your Project

You don't need to be famous.
But you do need to make your name *mean something* to the people who matter.

When people hear your name 10 years from now, will they say:

- "That's the person who changed my life"

- "That's the one who never quit"

- "That's who I want to be like"

Or...

- "What ever happened to them?"

- "Yeah, they had potential"

- "Didn't they fall off?"

**You decide.**

---

## Die Empty

This doesn't mean hustle until you collapse.
It means use what you've been given.

Don't die with:

- Unwritten books

- Unsung songs

- Unbuilt businesses

- Unspoken truth

- Unstarted projects

Give it all. Hold nothing back.
Die empty, not full of excuses.

---

## Legend Lesson

- Your legacy doesn't start when you're "ready." It starts today.

- Every act of discipline is a deposit in your future reputation.

- Don't aim to be liked. Aim to be remembered— for the right reasons.

---

## Mind Hack

Write your eulogy as if you died at 30.

What do they say about you?
What did you stand for?
Who did you impact?
What will echo after you're gone?

Now reverse-engineer that life.

---

## Trap Alert

Most people die full of "somedays."
Don't let distraction, comfort, or fear rob your last chapter.

You don't get to choose when you're gone.
But you *do* get to choose what you leave behind.

# Chapter 15: 10 Micro Habits That'll Change Your Life in 90 Days

*"Consistency is more important than intensity."*

-James Clear

You don't need a new personality You don't need to wait until you're "motivated."
You need **momentum**. And that starts with *one small win*—repeated.

Below are 10 micro habits. Each takes under 10 minutes.
Each will quietly rebuild your identity, day by day, until you become unrecognizable—in the best way.

---

## ☑ 10 Life-Changing Micro Habits (Grid Format)

| Habit | Time | Benefit | Replaces |
|---|---|---|---|
| 1. 10 Push-Ups on Wakeup | 30 sec | Kickstarts energy + discipline | Snoozing, apathy |
| 2. 1 Cold Shower Sprint | 3 min | Mental edge + stress resistance | Comfort addiction |

| Habit | Time | Benefit | Replaces |
|---|---|---|---|
| 3. "No-Scroll Morning" | 30 min | Clarity + emotional stability | Dopamine dependency |
| 4. Daily Truth Journal | 5 min | Self-awareness + mental hygiene | Avoidance, excuses |
| 5. Read 5 Pages | 10 min | Brainpower + vocabulary + vision | Scrolling, junk info |
| 6. 1 Task List w/ Priority | 3 min | Order + daily wins | Chaos, forgetfulness |
| 7. Compliment or Help 1 | 2 min | Leadership energy + confidence | Self-obsession |
| 8. No Complaining Rule | All day | Grit + control over emotion | Victim mindset |
| 9. 10-Minute Walk Alone | 10 min | Ideas + peace + perspective | Noise + anxiety |
| 10. Visualize Future Self | 2 min | Identity loop + belief growth | Drift, confusion |

## ✳ How Micro Habits Work (Why This Isn't BS)

- **Micro means repeatable.** You don't skip it. You don't negotiate.

- **Repeatable means compounding.** Each habit stacks momentum.

- **Momentum becomes identity.** And identity becomes destiny.

Let's break these down. You'll see why they work, how fast they hit, and how deep they change you.

---

## 1. 10 Push-Ups on Wakeup

**Why it works:** First act of the day = immediate discipline. It wakes your body anc signals that *you're in charge*.

**Challenge:** Every day. No matter what. Floor → 10 reps → conquer.

---

## 2. 1 Cold Shower Sprint

**Why it works:** This kills the comfort-first instinct. Forces your brain to breathe through stress. You walk out alert, sharp, and on edge—in a good way.

**Challenge:** Blast yourself for 60–90 seconds. Build up.

---

### 3. No-Scroll Morning

**Why it works:** Your brain wakes up fragile. Flood it with garbage and it *stays* weak all day. No phone for 30 minutes = clarity.

**Challenge:** Leave phone in another room overnight.

---

### 4. Daily Truth Journal

**Why it works:** One sentence of brutal honesty creates mental power. You stop lying to yourself. You stop drifting.

**Challenge:** One truth per day. Even if it hurts.

---

### 5. Read 5 Pages

**Why it works:** 5 pages/day = ~9 books/year. That's intellectual ammo. Books make you sharper, clearer, and harder to manipulate.

**Challenge:** Always know what your next book is.

---

### 6. 1 Task List with Priority

**Why it works:** Start your day on offense, not defense. Top 3 priorities—*in order*. Action breeds confidence.

**Challenge:** Write your 3 tasks before touching your phone.

### 7. Compliment or Help 1 Person

**Why it works:** Builds power by breaking self-obsession. Leadership = bringing energy, not stealing it.

**Challenge:** Do it without expecting anything back.

---

### 8. No Complaining Rule

**Why it works:** Complaining hardwires victim thinking. This rule forces you to reframe or stay quiet—and both build strength.

**Challenge:** Catch yourself. Rephrase into action.

---

### 9. 10-Minute Walk Alone

**Why it works:** Alone time = mental detox. No input, no phone. Just thoughts sorting themselves out. Like sweeping the mind.

**Challenge:** No distractions. Just walk. Just breathe.

---

### 10. Visualize Future Self

**Why it works:** You become what you see. Run a mental video of the version of you that *already made it*. Watch it until you believe it.

**Challenge:** 2-minute identity rehearsal. Daily.

---

### 🧠 Why 90 Days?

- You don't just change your habits.
- You **become the person** who never skips.
- You prove to yourself: *"I can be trusted to follow through."*

That self-trust? That's the foundation of everything.

---

### Legend Lesson

- The size of the habit doesn't matter. The **consistency** does.
- You don't rise to your dreams. You fall to your habits.
- Stack micro wins. Watch yourself evolve into someone dangerous—in the best way.

---

### Mind Hack

Print this list. Tape it to your wall.
Each habit, once per day. Cross them off.

Track 90 days. Post the before and after.
Let the results speak louder than your doubts.

**Trap Alert**

Waiting for motivation is a scam.

"Big changes" that never stick? Also a scam.

This is how you win: *daily decisions, zero drama.*

# Chapter 16: Build the Life You Want — No One Else Will Do It for You

*"The richest people in the world look for and build networks. Everyone else looks for work."*

-Robert Kiyosaki

Every chapter up to this point?

It's been a blueprint. A warning. A toolbox.

But none of it matters—**unless you move.**

Because here's the bottom line:

**Your life is your responsibility.**
Not your parents'. Not your school's. Not your friends'. *Yours.*

No one else is going to hand you freedom.
No one is going to hold your hand toward purpose.
No one is going to drag you up the mountain of your potential.

**That is your climb.**

---

## This Life Is Either Designed or Defaulted

You either *build* a life...
Or *end up* in one.

Default life means:

- A job you didn't choose
- A body you don't respect
- A partner you settled for
- A routine you resent
- A reputation you don't recognize

That's where drift leads.

Designed life means:

- You chose your standards
- You built your body, your money, your mindset
- You moved with intent
- You bled with purpose
- You lived by design—not reaction

**And the only difference?**
You took responsibility.

**No One Is Coming. You're It.**

This is your movie.
You are not a side character.
You are the writer, the director, and the main character all in one.

You choose the plot.
You choose the pace.

You choose whether this is a drama, a tragedy—or a goddamn revolution.

---

## The World Rewards Builders

Want freedom?

- Build habits
- Build value
- Build skills
- Build a name
- Build a body
- Build a system
- Build a future

**Builders rule the world.**
They're the ones who own their time, their thoughts, their results.

Everyone else is watching, waiting, consuming.

**You're not them.**
You're not average.
You're not soft.
You're not here to coast.

You're here to **build.**

---

**Legend Lesson**

- This is your life. Your responsibility. Your mission.

- If you want something better—*build it.*

- You don't get a second one. This is it. Make it count.

---

**Mind Hack**

Write this line where you'll see it every day:

**"No one is coming. I build."**

Repeat it until it's not just a sentence—it's your identity.

---

**Final Trap Alert**

The world is full of people who had potential and wasted it.
Don't become a story someone tells with sadness.

Become the one they point to and say: *"That's what it looks like to take full control."*

---

**Now go.**

You've got the blueprint.
You've got the vision.
You've got the fire.

**Build. The. Life.**

# Closing Charge: The Next 10 Years Are Yours

*"You don't get to win without losing first. That's the fee."*

-Darren Grimes

This isn't just a book.
This is a declaration of war on wasting your potential.

Because the truth is brutal and simple:
**No one is coming to save you.**
No teacher. No parent. No goverrment. No miracle.

If you want a future worth living, **you have to build it.**

You've been handed a cheat code disguised as work.
Discipline. Habits. Focus. Integrity. Direction.
You know the cost.
You know the reward.

So now what?

You can close this and scroll.
Or you can stand up and move like a damn weapon.

You can return to comfort.
Or you can enter the next 90 days like your name depends on it—because it does.

Forget who you've been.
Forget what you've done.
Forget what you've wasted.

**Today, you choose.**
To lead.
To sharpen.
To stack wins.
To walk like a king in the making.

Because the next 10 years?

**They either build a legacy—**
**Or bury a dream.**

You don't get both.

So get up. Get ruthless.
And build the life no one else will build for you.

**This is your time.**
Make them remember your name.

# THE 90-DAY CHALLENGE WORKBOOK

**Proof Over Potential**

*"The next 90 days will either change your life or reinforce your excuses. Choose wisely."*

**SECTION 1: BUILD YOUR BASELINE (PREP WEEK)**

**1. Life Audit: Where Are You Now?**

Rate yourself on a scale of 1–10. Be brutally honest. (1 = completely out of alignment, 10 = fully dialed-in and dominating)

| Category | Score (1-10) Notes |
| --- | --- |
| Discipline | |
| Energy | |
| Focus | |
| Purpose | |
| Identity (Clarity) | |
| Mental Diet Quality | |
| Emotional Control | |
| Finances | |

## 2. Hero Statement

**Prompt:** *"Who I will be 90 days from now..."*

Write a detailed vision of the version of you you're becoming. Include your daily habits, mindset, health, confidence, and results. Get specific: What time do you wake up? What are you proud of? What do others notice about you? What have you achieved?

## 3. Top 3 Goals (One from Each Category)

- **Physical:** (e.g., "Workout 5x/week" or "Lose 15 lbs")

- **Mental:** (e.g., "Read 3 books" or "Journal every day")

- **Creative/Financial:** (e.g., "Start a side hustle" or "Save $1,000")

## SECTION 2: MICRO HABIT TRACKER (WEEKLY)

**Instructions:** Check off each habit daily. Reset each week.

# DAILY HABIT TRACKER

| DAY | PUSH-UPS | READ 5 PAGES | NO SCROLL | TRUTH JOURNAL | VISUALIZE |
|-----|----------|--------------|-----------|---------------|-----------|
| Mon |          |              |           |               |           |
| Tue |          |              |           |               |           |
| Wed |          |              |           |               |           |
| Thu |          |              |           |               |           |
| Fri |          |              |           |               |           |
| Sat |          |              |           |               |           |
| Sun |          |              |           |               |           |

*screenshot, or download this page weekly*

## SECTION 3: 10 WEEKLY JOURNAL PROMPTS

Reflect every week using the question below. Use the space provided to write your response.

**Week 1:** What version of me needs to die for the next one to be born?

---

**Week 2:** What am I addicted to that's costing me my potential?

---

**Week 3:** What would my future self thank me for doing today?

---

**Week 4:** Where am I lying to myself?

---

**Week 5:** What hard thing am I avoiding that would make my life easier long-term?

---

**Week 6:** If I lived like I only had 2 years left, what would I change?

---

**Week 7:** Who do I need to forgive (or cut off) to move forward?

**Week 8:** When do I feel most alive?

**Week 9:** What toxic thought keeps looping in my mind?

**Week 10:** What kind of legacy am I building right now?

## SECTION 4: THE RESET RITUAL (SUNDAYS)

Take 10 minutes every Sunday to run this reset:

- What were my wins this week?
- What did I avoid, delay, or fail at?
- What is one simple shift I'll make this week?
- How will next week feel if I stay locked in?

*Use this ritual to calibrate weekly. No shame. Just data.*

## SECTION 5: THE BUILDER'S CODE

Sign this vow. Tape it up. **Read it aloud every morning.** Let it shape your actions.

**"I will not wait for permission.
I will not drift.**

I will build.
I will leave no potential unused.
I will die empty.
This life is mine to lead. And I will lead it."


**Signed:** _____
**Date:** _____


**You've got 90 days. Start now. And don't look back.**

www.ingramcontent.com/pod-product-compliance
Lightning Source LLC
Chambersburg PA
CBHW071207120626
46546CB00006B/2454